SOILED HANDS

&

BLISTERED FEET

TRUE STORIES LIVED AND WRITTEN
BY
TEDDY HODGSON

Edmund "Teddy" Hodgson
1898-1960

*"The Lord Jesus illustrated and commended a
Christianity that bent its back,* **soiled** *its* **hands**
and **blistered** *its* **feet** *in stooping to help fallen man.
Just as positively, He denounced and condemned a
professional religion that passes by on the other
side when man's need is at its greatest.
Some are called to be Apostles, but every
Christian is called to be an Epistle
(God's love letter, read of men)."*

Out of the Darkness. Victory Press. 1946

Table of Contents   *Pg*

Dedication

To the family of Edmund "Teddy" Hodgson.
His children; Peter, Michael, Christopher, Margaret, Ann.
His grandchildren; Robyn, Lynn, Helen, Onitha, Richard.
His great grandchildren; Emily, Oliver, Phoebe, Spencer,
Krystal, Natalie, Austin, Jordan, Noah, Isaac, Finn, Jotin.
And to future generations yet to be born, but who share in
our awesome legacy; a heritage of devotion, integrity and
honour because of our predecessor, Teddy Hodgson.

A Quick Word from Me

(Lynn Hodgson Riddick)

I never met my granddad; he died before my parents ever met.

However, I knew he had an effect on the world, when as a teen, some 20 years after his death, people would hear my last name and ask "Are you related to Teddy Hodgson?"

My granddad was a missionary in the Belgian Congo of Africa. He spent 40 years of his life in service to his God and to the Natives he loved so much. All 5 of his children were born there. (My dad would tell us stories of his childhood growing up in Africa: of the various animals he had as pets and the freedom he had to play and explore.)

Whenever he was home on furlough, Teddy would tell stories of his escapades. People spoke of what a great storyteller my granddad was. How the children would gather around him and listen as he told tales of hunting lions, marauding elephants and nasty crocodiles.

The stories in this book are Teddy's own words. I was originally going to edit them down and make them into a children's book, but I found that they lost a lot of their character and charm when I tried to re-arrange sentence structure, remove some of the wordiness, or try to make them less gruesome. These stories are of Teddy's hunting adventures and speak of blood, pain, and death, and so the idea of making a cute little children's book went out the window and instead you get Teddy pure and unedited.

My granddad was indeed a character with a big personality and so, in the end, I decided to keep the stories just as he wrote them. You can hear his accent. His personality, his charm, come through if you pause where he pauses and read as the punctuation dictates.
The spelling (for all of his American grandchildren) is good old English spelling.

Introducing Teddy
by David Womersley

Teddy Hodgson was larger than life.

A musketry instructor in the war and a cabinetmaker by trade. He studied at Thomas Mysercough's Pentecostal Bible School in Preston before joining the Congo (Zaire) Evangelistic Mission under W.F.P. Burton and James Salter in 1920.

He was a man full of laughter, love, strength and faith. A man's man, he fearlessly faced lions and elephants to protect frightened villages from death or starvation.

A gentle man, full of compassion, a man to be trusted.

A strong man when facing evil or pain.

An intrepid puller of teeth (without anesthetic), he flinched at nothing, even sewing up gaping wounds caused by enraged crocodiles or hippos. The people had infinite faith in his skills. He faced the most desperate of men - members of vile secret societies - to save girls sold into slavery or boys being tortured. He hated injustice from whatever quarter and detested slavery - his two books testify to this.

An excellent writer and story--teller, his illustrations were colourful, his similes striking.

He gave his time and his love unstintingly; he was generous to a fault.

Tragedy struck his life many times: he lost two wives and became a far-off father to his five children. How he loved and yearned for them! So he gathered around him surrogate black boys and girls.

A Bible student par excellence, he thrilled his audiences with his practical exposition of the Word. Tirelessly he opened up vast areas to the gospel, especially along the banks of the

Congo River, making his own boats for the task. When on leave, he brought missionary work alive. He spoke from his heart and moved many a congregation with his messages interlaced as they were with gripping stories.

He had become such a household name in Pentecostal circles that shock waves reverberated around the country at the BBC's sudden announcement of his untimely and violent death in November 1960.

Teddy closed his book "Out of the Darkness" with these words: "*The Lord Jesus illustrated and commended a Christianity that bent its back, soiled its hands and blistered its feet in stooping to help fallen man. Just as positively, He denounced and condemned a professional religion that passes by on the other side when man's need is at its greatest. Some are called to be Apostles, but every Christian is called to be an Epistle (God's love letter, read of men).*"

1
CONGO LIONS AND THEIR WAYS

It is easy in these days to pick up good hunting books and so very interesting to read of the great 'King of Beasts' and his ways in South Africa, Rhodesia, East Africa, Sudan and Somaliland, but my eyes are getting sore with looking for a printed record of Congo lions and their ways. Believing that "half a loaf is better than no bread", I am encouraged to write this little article. I have now lived for twenty years in the Congo and for twelve of those years have been keenly interested in lions, during which period, only occasionally and as an amateur; I have tracked, hunted and bagged thirty-eight lions, under all conditions, and mostly troublesome beasts. Always having followed them on foot, without dogs or even a second rifle, other that a twelve - bore shotgun carried by my boy. My own rifle is an old Le Metford .303.

We always allow that it is better to speak of people as we find them, so I am taking the same generous liberty with his feline Royal Highness, and shall speak of him only as I have found him in face-to-face encounters in Congo forests and plains. Facts are hard stubborn things and sometimes hard to swallow, always being more palatable when taken with a little fancy, so when I quote dry facts to guide my humble opinion, you can take my little experiences and findings as fancies, if you like.

One cannot meet this royal creature in his own domain without giving him every due respect and fear, not forgetting that he is the creature which, with our national modesty, we have selected as the emblem of our own valour and magnanimity. Who would dare to challenge such great authorities as the Natives themselves, with their rich animal folk lore, and amongst white men, General Sir Fredrick Lugard with his experience of all animals including the lion and the tiger, when they maintain the right of the lion to his title of 'King of Beasts?'

Here in the Congo the lion is left severely alone, by Natives in general, and hunters in particular. Though so unmolested, the Congo lion takes a heavy toll of domestic stock and Native life each year.

For many years, my nearest neighbor here in Congo, was a South African born professional elephant hunter. He spent more than half of each year away in the bush, shooting almost every species of animal without accident. Yet this hunter told me that he had never seen or met a lion in its natural haunts. He also confessed that he was so afraid of lions that he avoided every and any opportunity of meeting them. During my time up country here, I have known of many white hunters killed by buffaloes and elephants, but I do not know of one killed or mauled by a lion, for the simple reason that they have never tracked or hunted lions. I am sure that if they had hunted lions as freely as the buffalo or elephant there would have been more deaths. The Congo lion, given the same chances, could easily live up to the reputation given him by the highest authorities for killing, maiming for life, or badly mauling more men than any other species of hunted animal.

The renowned Selous shot over two hundred buffaloes, mostly on foot and under all conditions, without accident, and so regarded buffalo as not too dangerous. There is one thing sure and that is he could not have shot two hundred Congo lions under the same conditions. He would have been fortunate to have survived with even half that number to his credit. Personally, I have had more accidents or would-be accidents with buffaloes than with lions, and, after the lion, I heartily give the buffalo the credit of being the most dangerous adversary that a sportsman can engage.

11

In the north of Congo, a whole village of Natives was completely wiped out by lions. I grant that the victims were the most backward; living naked and not even making or carrying weapons in self-defense. Our own local lakeside village had once to be abandoned, the Natives living on the lake islands, because of a family of marauding lions which had taken possession each night. Their deliverance came by a traveling Native hunter, who came along well armed, to pay a visit. He found the village empty and it was too late to get away, so barricading himself in a hut he tried to rest. The lions scented him and started the siege. In sheer desperation, he pushed his muzzle-loaded gaspipe gun through the holes in the walls. Each time he felt a lion on the end of the gun he pressed the trigger. In the morning he fled from the village but left behind him several dead and

wounded lions, and the others changed their address and their hunting grounds.

Congo lions have a terrific appetite and are very destructive to game. When that is scarce, they destroy and devour domesticated animals, and when village animals are scarce, they prey easily on slow-witted humans. Amongst game, it is usually the male which they kill, as the male antelope generally takes the danger side, whether from hunter or lion; they loiter and invite trouble in order to let the herd get away. When I say that each lion on the plains eats daily one Lechwe or Puku antelope, the Natives who know, say that is far too modest a statement. The recorded facts go to show that one lion once killed a hundred pigs in an enclosure, in one night. Again one lion killed three camels in one day, and yet again fifty ostriches were killed in one night by lions in the fence, to say nothing of the slaughter of thirty sheep and goats in one night by lions; I should say angry, as well as hungry lions, angry at not finding the way out of the pen easily for stampeding, squealing pigs, goats, sheep and birds. I myself have found a lion killing and eating two big sheep in one night. Another time a lion killed and ate one goat, two dogs and eight ducks.

Here in the Congo, I believe that any and every hungry lion is liable to become a man-eater, not by habit or preference, but just because of sheer hunger when traveling from one hunting place to another, or when migrating to another place to give birth. All the Natives taken, killed and eaten by lions within my knowledge, were taken by traveling ones, which leave nothing or very little for identification purposes, being so hungry that often it is only just a hand or the back of the head and the torn loin cloth that is found. I knew of three man-eating lions killed by the Natives of three neighbouring villages on the river, in three successive weeks. In each case, the story and procedure were the same. The lion first attacked and killed a woman whilst gardening, then the drum called out all the Native men in the village to arm and to hunt down the lion. Hundreds of wild, shouting men surrounded the gardens and neighbouring bush, beating-up the lion, which, as the circle narrowed in, attacked the nearest man, at the same time being stabbed to death by scores of spears. The dead or dying man just being ignored and left to his relatives, the crowd triumphantly carrying their trophy back to the village. There to be sliced up into the smallest pieces and burnt publicly with great rejoicing and ceremony, as a wicked witch.

Only recently on the river, an expectant mother was sat outside her hut, feeding the slow fire that was smoking fish, when suddenly, without warning or noise, a lion walked up from behind, taking her neck in his huge jaws, he dragged her off to his two mates which were waiting only fifteen yards away under the banana palms. There they ate her, leaving nothing. The woman made no outcry at all, but was seen by the Natives at the next fish fire twenty yards away. Of course the next day the men folk followed up the lions, killed one and wounded another. I arrived too late for the lions but in time to render first aid to the only man mauled, and thus save his life.

I knew of a very sad and bad case that took place only twenty-five miles from here. The elephants were destroying the gardens so one Native, anxious to save his crops, went out and built three small huts in his garden, one for each of his wives at the ends and one for himself in the centre. One night the elephants did not come, so the drums and cans were silent, suddenly the man was disturbed by one of his wives crying out that there was a lion about. Then the other wife called out the same. As he got to the door of his hut, he saw the two lions meet, each dragging a wife in his huge jaws. The man was petrified with fear, his body and senses refusing to function, and he could only stay put and watch the brutes tear and devour his women. The next morning he was found almost demented and beside himself with grief.

I met another Native who, when a lion took his sleeping wife from his side one night, just got up to follow the lion and to die with his wife. Quite unconsciously and according to habit, he picked up his axe as he left the hut in the wake of the lion. As he overtook the brute with his wife, he struck out blindly with his axe and buried it deeply into the lion's skull, killing it on the spot. Then he awakened from his stupor. He had gone out to die in shame but came back into the village to enjoy countryside fame and glory.

Again, recorded facts go to prove that the King of Beasts is very tenacious to life; one lion not giving up the fight until it had been hit with thirteen bullets of various sizes from .303 to .450 plus seven S.S.S.G. shot cartridges. Yet another took six 10-bore, two .500, two .256 and three other bullets before he decided to quit this life. I should say the poor beasts died of lead poisoning. I myself cannot remember giving a lion more than three .303 bullets and one shot cartridge. Some I have got with one brain, neck, or spine shot; these are the only shots that will stop him in a charge. Even with a good heart shot, the lion is still good for a sixty-yard charge, or a longer run. A damaged lion soon succumbs to any serious wounds when he gets away, whereas an antelope very often recovers from even frightful wounds.

When the floods are on, they lay up on the ant-hills and parade the villages, serenading all the night with snarls, grunts and roars, until one half of the villagers are screaming in hysterics and the other half deadly silent, afraid to move or breath. I have known them to chase three armed white men out of the village into their boats; also, steamers have pushed off and moored in mid-stream by their fearful captains when lions have announced their presence. They are usually shameless and roar all night. It has now become a weird and wonderful fact, known all along the river, that when I visit the very same villages, they will not come near or roar within a mile of the place.

From my own observations, I believe that the lion does most of the hunting and driving, whilst the lioness does the killing. The male almost always walks on the open road, path or plain, whilst the females always walk parallel with him out of sight in the bush. By spoor, I have often read the story of the warning, the drive and the kill.

Lions on the plain never return to their kill. They eat bones, hide and meat, often leaving precious little for the attendant hyenas and vultures. Once hearing bones being crunched, I cautiously investigated, expecting to find hyenas. Imagine my surprise to find two lions that had eaten a whole lechwe, bones, meat and hide, leaving only the hooves, and were then chewing the last bit of bone at the end of the horns.

I have never found them following textbook methods of neatly disemboweling the animal, burying the entrails and commencing on the heart and other delicacies. I have found them biting lumps off the rump before tearing the victims open and then scattering the intestinal filth everywhere. I have also found them taking their fill of skin and bone, leaving plenty of good meat for the hyenas. On cutting up lions, I have found big pieces of bone, as big as my fist, also balls of hair in their stomachs. Their stool is always white and full of hair from part digested bone and hide.

The lion is supposed to have only one wife, but I usually come across him with two wives, one always older and bigger than the other one. They have lots of domestic squabbles, and their noisy quarrels often give their position away to the hunter. Also, the lioness's skin when obtained is well scarred with scratches.

I have come across lions in troupes of six or eight, and at the least grunt of alarm from one, they all close in to enquire. Congo lions do not seem to care what they tackle. I received the teeth and claws of one that had attacked a baby elephant and got killed and stamped on by the mother for his trouble. I was near on hand on two occasions, when lions attacked, killed and ate a hippo grazing on the riverbank. Lions here have sometimes been taken by crocodiles when swimming the channels. When Lechwe, Puku or Situtungu  antelope are driven into the water by men with dogs or by lions, the crocodiles waken up and move just in time to take the pursuer and not the pursued. Also, a lioness with cubs at one corner of the plain once killed six buffaloes.

My biggest surprise out here was to find that the lion cannot see very well on a dark night, but even if traveling along a road prefer to lay up until the moon rises or the stars break through: nearly all their killing is done just after sundown or just before daybreak. When the Natives first told me of the lion's immobility on a dark night, I laughed at them, but now find that they are right.

All the male lions here are maned according to age, and their colour ranges from light straw colour to a black-tinged tawny. The young lions are most deliberately spotted on the belly and legs, but as they get older these gradually disappear, but even on an older lion the spots are just discernible if you look hard enough.

Our Congo lions compare favourably with any I have seen in captivity in South Africa or elsewhere. I only remember measuring four of my trophies, of which the lions measured eight feet six inches from tip of nose to tip of tail, whilst the lionesses were only six inches less.

I have found lions to be real ventriloquists, controlling and throwing their voices about just at will. What used to appear to me to be a faint roar of a distant lion has often turned out to be the lion himself just the other side of the anthill. Whether he uses this definite and decided art for driving game, or just to misguide enemies, or both, I do not know yet.

For safety when unarmed in sight of a lion, I should always say pretend you have never seen him and move off at right angles, for they always remain silent and standing until your eye meets theirs, and then they either streak out in a charge, or else clear off in a shambling gallop. I have no faith in staring them out, for nothing irritates lions or leopards more than the human eye.

Yes, the Congo lion easily lives up to his hoary tribal reputation as 'King of Beasts' really fearing none save the human who is not afraid of him.

2
AN ADVENTURE WITH LIONS

As a youngster I remember the local docks professional rat catcher augmenting his official wages by keeping his biggest rats, extracting their teeth, then selling them for the training of young dogs, because the success of a terrier dog as a ratter depends such a great deal upon his first kill. If he makes an easy kill of his first rat, whose teeth have been drawn, he is never again afraid of rats. If, on the other hand, he gets badly bitten at his first kill, he is always handicapped through life by a lurking fear of rats. My first lion kill was very fortunate, so easy and such a good trophy, that keenness has been my great asset in every hunt since.

My first lion was the largest of three I fortunately spotted, without being seen by them, as they slouched along across the plain at about a hundred and fifty yards away. I got in a heart shot, and after a run of about a hundred yards he dropped dead. Since that wonderful day, all my kills have been more difficult, dangerous and exciting, but they have never robbed me of that feeling of mastery.

One of my earliest experiences with lions was late one afternoon. Lions were Public Nuisance No.1 in the village, and very troublesome on the plains, so I felt justified in looking them up.

I took with me three Natives who were not at all keen and who, also, were a little more inexperienced than myself. Two of them were sane sober hunters but the third was the village jester. He was as wide as he was long, and treated life as one huge joke. After getting away from the river with its big palm trees and dense undergrowth, we got out onto the plains where the grass was not too high, and you felt you had at least a hunter's chance of bagging something. After an hour's careful going, the boy spotted a lioness moving away from us in the distance. I was about to take a long shot at the disappearing target when the Natives begged me to make sure by getting nearer. I was furious when she disappeared into some dense bush undergrowth and left us sniffing around outside. I determined not to leave the spot until she came out, but after only a short wait with the sun already setting and darkness coming in fast, I reluctantly decided for the camp. I was carrying my old Le Metford .303 file with a sad heart, and the boys just behind me carried the shotgun, when just around the first big anthill we got the shock of our lives by running into five huge lions only sixty to eighty yards distant. They were as surprised as ourselves, and pulling up, stood stock still, head on, nothing moving except their tails in real anger. The Natives moved in behind me and hung onto my shirt in sheer fright. Shaking them off, I was galvanised into the super-rapid thinking and acting, I decided to hit quick and hard all around. As never before, I appreciated to the fullest my army training in rapid loading and aiming. Five shots rang out and five lions dropped like ninepins with wicked pig like grunts. That was the first time I learnt to record when a lion was a hit or a miss. At such good fortune, I felt hilariously intoxicated, but nearly froze with fear when all the five huge beasts got up and decided to come for me. Before, when standing head on with swishing tails, they looked savage enough, but now they looked positively ugly and wicked as they came on as best they could with bared claws and fangs. Now at about twenty paces I fired at all five lions again, four were recorded grunting hits and one a whistling miss. Two huge maned lions dropped less than ten paces away, and only by snatching the shotgun from the boy and firing immediately was I able to drop the biggest lioness at five to six paces away. All three, as they dropped, bit huge holes in the hard baked clay of the plain. The remaining two wounded lions made a terrific noise behind the anthill as we slowly backed out of action into safety, for we had not another cartridge left and it was almost too dark to see, even to retreat.

The whole way back to the village, and later around the campfire that night, not one of those three Natives spoke a word, but their silence spoke volumes to the enquiring Natives. That night I hardly slept a wink for excitement, and found it not difficulty to get up at half past four the next morning to dig out my reluctant Natives. It was too dark to see, but I expected it would be light enough by the time we got near to the three trophies. I had never reckoned on the wounded lions waiting about for me. As it got lighter, a heavy mist fell on the plains and we could not see at all. So getting near, as we thought, we spread out so as not to miss the place. The little fat village jester got out on one flank and as he fearfully advanced disturbed one of the wounded lions, for it gave a terrible roar. It was serious indeed, but we nearly died with laughing to see the jester with all the jest taken out of him, running for dear life to hide behind me, his knees going up and down like pistons.

We had to pull up and wait for seven o'clock, until the sun was up high enough to dissolve the mist, then we saw the three lions with their mouths filled and wedged open by their bites into mother earth.

The country around was ideal, the grass short, trees absent except on the anthills, and these anthills punctuated the whole landscape. We knew that one of the wounded lions was hiding in the wooded shelter of one of these hills, but which one we could not tell as we had quite lost our bearings in the mist and the lioness kept severely quiet. Feeling more courageous in the sunshine we extended into open order and advanced cautiously, keeping a reasonable distance away from anthills. I took the flank on which we decided she was, and the jester took the flank where he was sure she was not. We had not advanced far before, from the anthill nearest the jester, out came a terrible angry roar that sent him pistoning along my way again. Now we had located the dangerous beast, but the trouble was, to see her let alone get her. She could look out perfectly but we could see nothing of the inside of her retreat. Sending two of the men away to safety I took the remaining and best Native to reconnoitre the thickly wooded anthill. We circled the place twice at a reasonably safe distance but could not see or hear anything, so we crouched down for observation. I had just decided to try and drive her out with a chance shot when the Native nudged me, drawing my attention to a hardly discernible whitish object - not unlike a faded leaf behind the green ones. He declared that he had seen it move. So believing him, I took careful aim at the target, which proved to be the lioness's bared fangs. She shot right up into the air above the foliage and dropped back stone dead with most of her teeth smashed.

A big storm was coming on so we hastened to put our four fine trophies together, investigate and photograph them, before getting down to skinning. On examination, I found that four of the first shots were indeed fortunate; penetrating the chest, hitting the spine in the lumbar region and paralyzing the hindquarters. This had stopped them from springing or charging in the usual way. They just clawed themselves along to me with their powerful fore quarters until the second head or neck shot dropped them stone dead. The wounded lioness that gave us the thrills had been hit in the chest, but just to one side, the bullet passing out behind the shoulder. So she still possessed her dangerous springing or charging powers until the mouth shot deprived her of all, even after thoughts.

After photographing and skinning the four lions, we 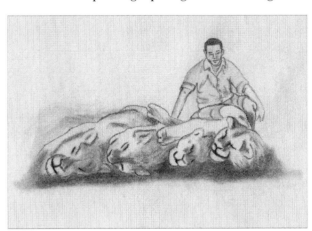 just got back to the village as the storm broke. The next day Natives returned from across the plain, found the fifth lion dead and part eaten by vultures. He had been hit in the chest and spine, but had managed to drag himself out of our sight and away. There the scavengers of the sky announced his death.

The two lions measured eight feet six inches from tip to tip and the lioness managed to reach the eight feet measurement. They being the only four of my thirty-eight lions that I have ever measured.

3
ANIMALS THAT DREAM DREAMS

I feel inspired on this subject today and can write quite feelingly, for my feet are blistered and all my bones ache after an unsuccessful day hunting elephants. Now there is not a single possible human reason why I should have drawn a blank today, for I did not sleep in the village or vicinity, but arrived very early and unexpectedly. Also, the elephants had not changed their habits or haunts for months. But today, the one and only day, when death was possible, they raided the gardens as usual and then at daybreak, like the Wise Men after their warning dreams, went home another way, leaving me to scramble around where they ought to have been, whilst they calmly crossed the river to a safe retreat.

Getting back into the village, the Chief, old men, and hunters all greeted me with the inevitable welcome. "Yes Bwana, the elephants dreamed of death last night, and took the warning to leave so as to live to maraud another day."

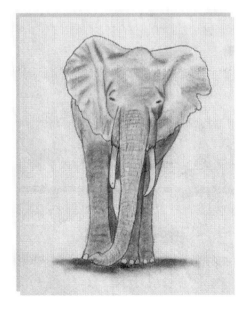

In my younger days, feeling clever, I used to laugh and call it ignorant superstition, but now I know that the Native expresses in a simple way what I myself have learnt to believe after much experience.

Most decidedly all wild life is uncannily sensitive to invisible guidance and control. Their migrating, mating and breeding is not left to mere chance or their choice. The same unseen force that gives them time and direction leadings, with mass unheard thinking also warns them individually of danger. Of course this sounds silly to the materialistic minded, and only to be expected from those who live lives far divorced from nature. Generations of luxurious living in artificial surroundings have dulled our ordinary God given senses, until in some cases they have ceased to function at all. In fact, some of us are so full of beef and unbelief, that the only spirit we can believe in is that out of a bottle. On the other hand, primitive people become so much natures own children, that their every sense becomes acutely sensitive so that they become naturally spiritual and sense their way through life. So how very much more so the hundred percent wildlife, whose very existence often depends on the use of its senses.

Sportsmen casually say that they see their best game when they carry no gun. The Native hunters also say, "It is not us armed men that see the game, but our harmless womenfolk, when out gathering firewood." I would even go one better and say, "It is not the hunter, or the gun that he carries that stampedes the animals, but his intention to kill". My own experience is that when I am solely following lions or their spoor, the other animals do not bother to get out of my way. But the very moment that I decide the hunt is over and it is time to shoot one antelope for the boys, then and only then, do the antelope take alarm and stampede to safety.

In actual practice I have tried out all the reasons, explanations and excuses put forward by reasonable authorities and find that they all are a bit of truth, but the Native is nearer the whole truth, when he says that they dream dreams. What does it matter whether they are night dreams, daydreams, or just hunches; they are certainly spiritual warnings that give wild animals the proverbial "cats nine lives" as these few experiences will go to prove.

Before I was interested in shooting lions, you could set your calendar if not your clock by their inevitable and punctual visits to my house and district. Shamelessly they shook the houses and beds with their roaring, scaring the dogs into a dead silence but sending the womenfolk into hysterics. From the very day that I took a more than ordinary interest in their skins, they altered their time immemorial route and now silently make a detour around the mountain two miles always.

To this day on the river, there are some villages that the lions terrorise at certain months of the year, by occupying them all night to feast on goats, dogs, ducks and occasionally a Native. In all these villages I am a very welcome and honoured guest, for then the Natives are guaranteed a good night's sleep, as the lions will not come within a mile of the village and even then will be careful not to roar. This is not an exception, but the absolute rule now.

In one village they begged me to stop, as two families of lions were troubling them and had been doing so for over a month. The Natives were afraid to go to their gardens in the daytime and had to barricade themselves in their huts at night. Hiding the boat out of the village, I started my hunt half past four in the afternoon. But at eight that night returned tired and disappointed. Not a squeak did we hear all night, so I was off again on the hunt at eight o'clock the next morning, but had to return at nine o'clock, not having seen or heard anything. Just then, a Native came in from across the plains and reported that he had seen the two families of lions swimming the channel to clear the district. There was one family of five and one of six lions. Knowing where they would make for, I set off in pursuit before they had time to dream again. Sure enough, I came upon the family of six in the most impossible bush. All of them were big brutes but I bagged five of them. Only their old man got away.

Once calling at another village, the Chief begged me with tears in this voice to stay the night, as a family of lions had cleared the whole village of dogs and goats. Only one goat remained and he feared for his people. The brutes shamelessly tore and devoured the goats right on the house verandahs, whilst the natives screamed in terror. I saw for myself that the whole village and gardens were padded with lion spoor and even the hut walls, doors and thatch were well damaged by the revelrous beasts. Hiding the boat well out of the village at sunset, I took up my vigil in the hut alongside the goat house that contained the village's last and only goat. The lions always roared before sundown as they left their retreat further up the riverbank. But that night I was not even encouraged with that roar. From sundown until midnight I suffered agony from the clouds of mosquitoes and the vile smell of the over seasoned goat house. Then silently I returned to the boat to listen from there, but was not rewarded with a sound or a sight of lions all night. Next morning, on making a reconnoitre of the village I found that the lions had approached the village to within one mile and then made a big detour.

At this very same village, I called again and berthed the boat quite openly, as I could not hunt or shoot since I had not a single cartridge for either rifle or shotgun. I was absolutely harmless and the lions knew it well, for two of them serenaded me the whole night. At daybreak I spotted the pair of them on an anthill at less than one hundred yards. On sight of me they gave one big defiant roar and disappeared into the papyrus swamp.

On yet another occasion, whilst travelling on the river I saw a wounded antelope escape a Native hunter, by taking to the river and swimming across. Just as it arrived at the other side, it was taken by a huge waiting crocodile. Being angry at such a dirty trick, I swung the boat round and made at full speed for the struggling antelope.

The crocodile only just saved his life in time by letting go his prey. Grabbing the antelope, I dragged it on board, but it was already dead. At the next village, the lonely trader complained bitterly of sleepless nights because of roaring lions that would not move along. Making enquiries from the Natives, I found that there were two families of lions that met nightly to make love and whoopee in the big sweet potato patch behind the village. This they had done nightly for weeks. Knowing their objection to strange scent, I let the Natives fix the dead antelope for bait in the middle of the potato patch. After first bleeding it and sprinkling the blood across all the many converging lion trails through all the long grass. Everything was just perfect for a good lion kill. Just after sundown, one lion gave a warning grunt about half a mile away and that kept all the others away and silent all night. The boys cut up and ate the untouched bait the next day before it suffered any more deaths or indignities.

These are only a few amongst many experiences that convince me of something spiritual, beyond the generally understood sixth sense of protection that animals have and that is lost in man. No, their ordinary five senses, even when so acute and sensitive as to be beyond all human apprehension and appreciation, cannot possibly account for all their deliverances from planned death by man. Surely the Native is the nearest to the whole truth when he says that they "DREAM DREAMS" and live.

4
DO LIONS CLIMB TREES?

It just depends on what you call climbing. For it is
certain that they are occasionally found in trees. The biggest
and finest specimen of a maned lions that I have ever bagged
was high up in a tree.

Nobody doubts or questions the ability of the agile
leopard to climb trees. Here on the Congo River they even
climb fifty to sixty feet bare stemmed palm trees. During the
months when the river floods, they live and sleep in the big
deciduous trees, often taking their kill with them. And this is
frequently an animal larger than themselves. The smaller of
the two big cats we always expect to be as much at home
climbing trees as stalking through the bush, but his four to
five times bigger cousin, the lion, we feel, does not possess the
same capacity. But after having seen a thrice-wounded lion
charge at the speed of an express train, after having seen a
lion clear at one leap a fifteen feet obstacle, I could almost
give him credit for flying. No, I should not say the lions climb
trees, but I should say that he just leaps into a suitable tree
and uses it as an observation post without being observed
himself.

Just as the household tabby cat sharpens hits claws on
the table leg, so does the lion sharpen its claws in the same
way on the tree trunk. Often in lion country I have seen the
family grindstone, a tree trunk badly clawed about five feet
from the ground.

On one occasion, I visited a village near the plains
and found the Natives in great fear of two lions that had just
come down from the mountains. The people were
accustomed to the usual plain dwelling lion that stalks in the

open and makes his kill by his super speed. But these two new lions preferred the bush along the edge of the plain, where they waited in trees to prey on the game.

As I was very interested, I sent my Native tracker to scout along the edge of the plain, whilst I myself took the Native path in the bush with another Native, in order to intercept the lions as they left their lair to come to the plain. After a while, the tracker I had left along the edge of the plain came tearing along, all excitement and perspiration, saying he had seen the biggest lion of his life. Its size had scared him. He said it looked like a buffalo, being big and dark of colour. I followed him hard, warning him to stop and give me time to take my breath just before we arrived at the place where he had seen the lion. We got to the fringe of the plain but kept hidden in the trees. The boy looked around in dismay, saying: "Bwana, he has gone, but where?" The plain was one bare expanse, with just one tree standing like a sentinel. I felt very disappointed, until the boy excitedly whispered that the lion was up in that tree. I could see nothing but thick foliage, so I stalked against the wind and got as near the tree as possible. Still I could see nothing, so I asked the boy where it was and where its head and where its tail were supposed to be. He knew instinctively how the great beast was lying and where it was looking, so he gave me a general idea of where to shoot. I did shoot with the idea of getting him out of the tree and onto the plain so as to get a second and surer shot, but the first was a lucky shot that broke his back, which of course, I did not know until later.

I saw him reach out of the tree with his huge forepaws and drag himself down to the ground.

His paralysed hindquarters hung over a branch like a big clothes peg, whilst he grunted in rage, tore at the tree trunk, until at last his hindquarters unhooked themselves off the branch, and let him fall in a heap at the base of the tree. From there he shuffled around and sat up on his dead haunches, then like a huge mastiff, angrily faced me, looking formidable with his bared fangs, and sounding terrible with his grunting roars of rage. In fact, he looked so unwounded and aggressive that I took a quick brain shot, which he fortunately got. What a magnificent specimen he was! I took my helmet off to him in admiration and respect, for he was the biggest and bonniest dark maned lion that I had ever seen. Not being altogether satisfied, I went to look for his wife the next day. She saw me first as I approached from the plain, so all I saw of her was her huge body leaping down from the tree and disappearing into the bush.

On another occasion, a full-grown male lion, badly wounded, after charging at me twice, and bleeding like a stuck pig, leapt up into a tree and lay there for a long time waiting for me to follow up his spoor. Fortunately, I was delayed some long time bandaging up my gun boy whom this lion had mauled in his charge, so I only arrived after the lion had descended from the tree to go off into the thicket to die. The big pools of blood on the ground and the bloodstains on the tree trunk and branches told their own tale of amazing feline agility and ability.

Now I know lions don't apologetically climb trees, but that they take them in their stride when it suits their purpose.

5

MY FIRST EXPERIENCE WITH LOVE SICK LIONS

A real overdose of humour and excitement came into my first thrilling encounter with lovesick lions. Even the King of Beasts loses some of his dignity when the love bug bites him. He appears to forget what he got up for or where he is going. Love even blinding his eyes to the presence of vulgar onlookers, whom he unconsciously attracts and entertains. Also, he becomes deaf to the cry of his own empty belly.

At the time of the incident, I was not out particularly for hunting, but was visiting the temporary dry season fishing camps on the plains. I had made fast the motor boat at one of the most convenient river villages. My rifle was useless with a broken trigger spring, but being Sunday the next day, I refrained from making the repair so as to avoid any temptation to shoot on the Sabbath whilst crossing the plains.

That night I was awakened by the most hideous pantomime of noise. It was so fiendish and unusual that it took me some time to place it. Then I recognised it as a crowd of hyenas laughing. Their manacle laughter was contagious and I soon found myself also laughing and heard the Natives in the nearby huts laughing as well.

The more the hyenas laughed the more I became inquisitively intrigued to know at what they were laughing. Being unable to sleep any more with such a chorus going on, I got up at four thirty to follow and find out the cause of such persistent hilarity.

I dug one boy out of bed to go with me, telling the others to strike camp at sunrise, pack the loads and take the usual trail across the plain to the other side. There we would meet them later in the day. I did not intend to shoot at all, but took the dislocated rifle along, as it could bang off an alarm if wanted, even if it was impossible to shoot anything that needed any aim taking at it.

It was dark, cold and wet as we set off, and we became even wetter as we crossed the channels of water; parted the long dewy grass; fell into and scrambled out of unseen holes for the better part on an hour; but the continued madhouse cackle kept us on a straight course out into the bare plain.

It was still dark and we could only just discern the big isolated trees and anthills. Soon however, the boy pulled up short, got down on his tummy, for he had actually located the nocturnal revellers. Getting down myself and using the lighter sky as a background, I too could see a prancing ring of eight hyenas. There being no cover between us, we advanced slowly on our tummies to some fifty or sixty yards from the hyenas, and further we could not go, for the big lechwe antelope had fixed us with his eyes. He was only ten yards away and appeared unable to run for it.

Our crawling seemed to intrigue him more than the octet chorus party, for he could only look in our direction and nervously stamp his feet in alarm. When day was dawning, we could just see enough to enjoy the strange animal pantomime. It was indeed great fun to see the ungainly brutes hopping about, up and down and laughing like demons.

Soon the boy warned me that the attraction in the centre was a lion. I strained my eyes and sure enough, there was the beast. Then the boy whispered in alarm that he could see two lions. A little more concentrated observation on my part enabled me to discern two large lions. After, when it became lighter, we could see that they were not eating but lovemaking.

Then I knew what the hyenas were laughing about, and nearly laughed myself in sympathy. Being cowardly scavengers and not courageous killers, they were trying to laugh their lord and master out of love making to make kills to satisfy their hungry bellies.

When daylight added ugly faces and fantastical animal forms to the laughing gatecrashers, the lions objected and we watched breathlessly as the two lions in turn took to chasing and driving the eight hyenas in every direction, sometimes dangerously our way.

The intruders scattered like quicksilver, only to return, laughing and reforming their ridiculous ring around the courting couple.

Sanity and normality seemed to return with the sunrise, for the King of Beasts and his wife arose, shook themselves, stretching their necks in a look around for a kill. Their gaze was arrested in our direction for they spotted the antelope that was still stamping its feet in nervous apprehension as he failed to understand our unusual and immobile forms at such close quarters.

As one of the lions crouched to stalk the hypnotized antelope I whispered to the boy not to move a hair or he would spoil the game, for we were going to see an unusual sight. He moved more than a hair as he looked back for a way of retreat, and saw two big elephants coming on at good pace with their huge ears flapping and trunks waving.

His movement broke the spell for the antelope and sent it streaking off at right angles. This in turn caused the lion to straighten himself and swish his tail in defiance, as he looked our way. The boy tried to look both back and front at the same time as he pleaded with me to get him out any way except toward the oncoming elephants.

The gun could still bark even if it could not bite, so I tried to aim at the lion but the bullet hit the ground some yards in front of him, having no more effect than causing the animal to look extremely disgusted as he turned around and sauntered back to his mate. Then both animals just loped off a few yards and sat down like two great mastiffs to look at us. But you could not see the hyenas for dust, so perhaps after all the lions felt a little thankful for our intrusion if it was only to scare of the graceless and vulgar nightlong serenaders.

We retreated to one side and then saw that the two big elephants were only the leaders of quite a large heard of visiting elephants that the drought had driven riverwards. The boy told a great tale when we got to camp that day and so impressed the others that they held a council of war, the result of which was to send a deputation to me saying ...

"Yes Bwana, the lions were legitimately courting, but you yourself were unnecessarily courting trouble, so for our sakes will you please not do it again."

Of course, I promised not to do it again -

until next time.

6

THE EXPERIENCE WAS UNFORGETTABLE,
BECAUSE . . . .

I WAS LITERALLY PARALISED WITH FRIGHT

"Paralysed with fright" and "Petrified with fear" are no longer just paltry figures of speech to me as they were, until quite recently, when I laughed at these sayings, which I called "mere exaggerated terms of expressive language." Now I know it to be an actual physical experience, never to be erased from one's memory.

War escapades and mad hunting escapades have invariably found and left me reasonably cool, calm and collected, with fear only lurking in the background. Now, through one recent and never-to-be-forgotten experience, I know what it is to be positively still with fright, conscious but unable to move a muscle in self-help, or even articulate one sound until the danger was past. Now I am glad that this part of my life's education was not left to a bad dream, nightmare or any of man's devices or mechanical contraptions, or even to a lesser animal than the King of Beasts himself, and that at the most majestic and defiant of his life when, with teeth, mouth and claws dripping with the hot blood of his kill, he belched forth his earth-vibrating roar of defiance to the whole world. All this took place on a tropical stormy night.

This is how it all happened. It was the end of the dry season, when the once-flooded plains become punctuated with dried gaping fissures and mud pools. Then the rivers have become rivulets, and all the water channel-connections between the plains and Congo River become just hard-baked highways for meat-hungry Natives to trek along to cut-off and imprisoned fish in the pools and mud holes. In this no-man's land hundreds of Natives congregate, build temporary fishing camps, feed well and become rich as they trap, spear, and collect tons of fish to sell to White traders, who in turn send it down to the mining camps.

As my labours take me wherever Natives are found, they often find me in their outlandish fishing and hunting camps on brief visits. This time I had struck one of their biggest camps and found lots of old friends. In the distance, their camp of some 200 huts looked like a real oasis in the midst of a wilderness of hard-baked mud, but as I got nearer the riot of smells just shrieked at me, meat in every stage of freshness, rottenness and cooking. Those without firewood smoked their fish on buffalo-dung fires, to put the special kipper taste into their herrings. Others without firewood or dung just left the meat to rot in the water and then hung it up everywhere to bake white in the sun. The stench was unbearable, so I selected a site for my tent well out of the village on the side where the fresh air breezes were coming from. In the distance, a herd of lechwe antelope was grazing, and in the immediate vicinity, there was lots of fresh lion spoor. These things I hardly noticed, as I was so keenly interested in watching the Natives using all their community weight and ingenuity in catching all sorts of mud and fresh water fish. It was a scream to follow them as they walled off portions of the pond with portable reed fences, then up to 100 Natives would jump into the muddy water and start to drive with legs, arms, spears and bottomless basket traps with a hand-hole in the top by which to extract the unlucky fish when the basket flopped down into the mud. They had some resemblance to monkeys as they trailed behind them a long tail of rope on which to thread their fish as they caught them.

They slipped and flopped into the water so often themselves, screaming as the fish wriggled to get from under their anatomy or jumped up and hit them in the face. They reminded one forcibly of a fat man sitting in a bath, feeling around for the soap. All this excitement and then staying onto the bitter end to watch the important owner of the pond, sitting at the outlet, taking 50 percent of everybody's catch as his share for letting them paddle in the mud hole that he had inherited from his forebears. Only then, on getting back to the tent, did I realise what a long way I was out from the village. The antelope drawing in nearer to my tent told me plainly that there were lions about, and that they were afraid of them. It was too late to make enquiries or preparations, and not being unduly fearful, I left the tent ends open as the heat was so oppressive and warned me of a coming storm.

After supper, being all alone, I placed my rifle handy in one corner of the tent, put the matches, lamp and cartridges ready on the chair, and noticed the place of everything ready for a quick get-out in case of lions coming along. Soon the storm broke in all its fury, and quietened all life down to an awed hush. Before going to sleep, I closed up the foot of the tent against the rains, but left the verandah-end wide open. Being healthily tired, I was soon asleep, until the shock came about midnight.

I was rudely awakened by the mighty roar of a lion right in the tent. The bed and ground were shaking, and the tent and air just vibrated as if a bomb had exploded. I wakened to a world where everything was vibrating except myself. My eyes were open. I knew what had taken and was taking place, but I was pathetically helpless, and could not wink an eye, move a muscle or make a squeak. I just lay there, ridiculously helpless and hopeless, waiting for the lion to collect me without a protest. Then I heard him drag his kill off the tent ropes, and as he drew off the use of my limbs returned and I felt angry at having missed such a chance. It was still raining, and I was too shaken to attempt anything further that night, apart from closing the front of the tent and trying to go to sleep again.

Illustrated by H. Marriott-Burton for "The Outspan" May 29 1942

What had actually happened was that the fearful antelope had gathered very close round my tent after dark, when the lion struck his victim down in his spring he scattered the herd, and they, falling over the many tent ropes, caused the tent to sway and flap ominously. This being so unusual and unfamiliar, irritated the lion, so that he roared out his defiance, this terrific volume being caught up under my tent-fly, nearly bursting my eardrums. Seeing there was no response from the tent, His Majesty just dragged his kill off to a more congenial place to share it with his mate.

The next morning I felt thoroughly ashamed of myself and tried to account for the involuntary fear that was absolutely paralysing. I could only put it down to one thing, and that was, that being so perfectly relaxed in deep sleep that the sudden earthquake of a noise only wakened my mind, and so shocked it that it could not function to waken my limbs. Normally a lion's roar at night is music to me, and the nearer the better; waiting up for them, going out to meet them at dusk and even dark is the spice of life to me, and it never before found me lacking in presence of mind, but this monarch not only robbed me of my presence of mind but of the use of my limbs as well.

Anyway, what I lost in reputation and trophy that night I made up for the next day by tracking and hunting and bagging a huge maned lion who had made himself Public Enemy No. 1 by preferring to frequent Native paths and villages to his own wild domain.

After making many inquiries amongst the Natives, I find that is quite a common thing for them to be paralysed with fear or to scream in uncontrolled hysteria when the King of Beasts acclaims himself too near their huts at night.

Now I can understand how shock and fear can be paralysing, and I can also be more sympathetic with those more nervous than myself.

7

SOME THRILLS OF LEOPARD HUNTING IN THE CONGO

Leopards are less than one-third the size of lions. The record leopard shot was only the weight of a ten-stone man. They will fly at a man readily and viciously on slight provocation or no provocation at all. They bite and scratch in a nasty way, generally about the face and shoulders. The biggest danger from their attack is blood poisoning. In hunting them there is little danger to life or limb, as they cannot brain a man at one stroke, or crunch and break big bones as the lions generally do. As they are under the average weight of a man, they can be brained with a club or strangled with bare hands - if the person attacked keeps his presence of mind.

Leopards are most decidedly more silent than lions, also more strictly nocturnal, not leaving their lairs until after dark and returning before dawn; that is why so few are shot in fair sport. Also, if they are disturbed at all, they can creep away unseen giving no chance for a shot.

Leopards are much more suspicious than lions, and are consequently difficult to draw to bait, as they examine trees and bush everywhere for suspicious foreign scents. They are also difficult to catch on their kill, as they invariably drag their meat into the thicket to eat. To their credit, we must record the fact that they can drag a victim heavier than themselves fifteen feet up into a tree. I have never heard of a man-eating leopard, and contrary to some authorities, I have found them hunting and living in the same terrain with lions.

My first interest in leopards came when one attacked a local Native as he went along the bush path. He was carrying his spear, so he pierced the huge cat, nailing it to the ground and then stamped its ribs in with his feet. Not many months afterwards, the same Native set a gun trap to catch a marauding leopard. He hid himself not far from the gun. When he heard the gun go off and then saw the leopard getting away unwounded, he forgot himself, and just threw himself at the beast and strangled it with his bare hands! He was badly mauled, but no bones were broken, and no harm would have come to him if he had been treated, but, having enemies in the village, he was more than neglected, and so he died from blood poisoning.

I have doctored lots of Natives attacked and mauled by leopards, but have never known a fatal case yet, except the one recorded.

Several times I have taken kills made by leopards and heard them slink away at my approach without giving me the slightest sight for a shot. I have stalked the same antelopes with leopards without seeing them, but my boys did. I have also heard them stalk their prey and make their kill in the swamps.

Here is another strange thing: I have never yet found a boy that would point out a leopard to me when out hunting. They evidently think that there is more chance of a canine mauling than there is chance of a shot, so they wait until you get back to camp to tell you what their keener eyes have seen, much to your disgust.

In the daylight I have caught glimpses of them in retreat, and even seen them drinking at the river, but without the chance of a shot, so the only leopards which I have bagged have been at night when marauding in the villages.

Here is my most exciting experience with a leopard at night. The boat was tied up at the riverbank, and as it was nine o'clock at night, I was enjoying the campfire with the Natives. Suddenly I was roused by the ominous grunt of a leopard in the papyrus swamp. The Natives told me that he was a big old leopard, which had no fear of man, and regularly raided the village for dogs, goats, ducks and fowls. I dashed into the boat to get my .303 rifle and a small carbide headlamp and set off to find the beast, who still kept up his grunts. The village was built on a raised dry bank only twenty feet wide, so that when I stepped into the papyrus I went up to my waist in water and could not see a thing but a solid wall of green papyrus. Coming back disappointed and wet, I thought out a plan as the leopard grunted again higher up. I knew he was walking parallel to the village, and that if I continued along the path on the higher bank we would meet sooner or later. As he grunted and advanced in the swamp, I kept in line with him on the bank, until after quite a distance I spied an opening in the papyrus where somebody had made a bit of a clearing for gardening. Suddenly I spotted two red flames exactly like the flames of a Native fire, which flare up when the pot is lifted off.

My boy whispered, "Shoot, Bwana, shoot!" but I dare not, as I actually believed that it was a Native campfire. Anyway, to make sure, I turned the light away and looked again in the dark and, instead of the flames going out, as I expected they should do if it was the leopard, they only died down slowly, just as a Native fire would do when the cooking pot is replaced on the flames. Next, I heard the leopard grunt and jump, and then I knew it was indeed the leopard I had seen. The boy assured me that there was not a campfire within a mile in that direction, so I went on after him. When he turned around, I got his eyes again, the same two wavering red flames; as soon as I got the sight, he got the shot and never knew what hit him.

The bullet struck him right in the teeth that were bared in defiance; not even singeing his lips or whiskers, then broke his neck, and finally lodged in the fat just under the skin at the back of the neck. He dropped stone dead without a movement or grunt and we carried him back to camp, the biggest leopard seen in this part of the world. Only two teeth remained whole in his mouth, so the local chief came along to beg them. I gave them to him on condition that he told me why he wanted them. He said he wanted them to tie to the necks of his hunting dogs as charms against leopards, as he had lost so many of his dogs to them whilst hunting situtungu in the papyrus swamps.

When the river is in flood, the leopards lay up in the huge trees along the banks. It is impossible to see them, but if you fire a shot cartridge into the foliage when passing, the leopards streak down and disappear into the papyrus and rank grass. Sometimes there are as many as thirteen in one tree.

I knew of one White trader up this way who developed a real leopard complex, never going out after dark, and barring all his windows and doors at dusk. All this happened after a terrifying experience with a leopard. He was cycling along the motor road cut through the bush. It was just getting dusk when a big leopard came out of the undergrowth, made a circle around him and then disappeared into the bush. He was afraid and cycled hard, but the leopard followed unseen in the bush, appearing again and circled around him, only much closer. Then he cycled for dear life, but the leopard appeared again ahead of him, this time knocking against his cycle, and disappeared again. Just then, a motor car came along and stopped for the now distracted man, and took him aboard. The leopard came yet again and was shot dead by the car owner, who fixed him with the headlights. I have heard of one missionary who has bagged about eighty leopards at night by lamp and gun and come off unscathed, so, taking all facts into consideration, I think we have over-estimated the danger from the killing power of our lovely feline friend.

8

MY MOST EXCITING LION HUNT, THE MEMORY OF WHICH I CAN NEVER FORGET

In hunting and shooting some forty odd lions of every kind and under all circumstances, I have alternately enjoyed and endured some strange sensations and experiences; from an exciting running fight at five to seven hundred yards, to a frightful stand-up fight at only five to seven yards. From dropping a cowardly retreating lion at long distance, to stopping a ferocious, charging one at only a few yards. From foolhardily following them on hands and knees through mere tunnels in the dense grass and bush growth, to finding them enraged and bleeding waiting to attack me from the branches of overhanging trees. From killing them from vantage places, to dropping them whilst worrying my own gun-boy at my very feet. From stalking in safety with two guns, well loaded and good boys, to being found alone face to face with them, wounded, at only two yards with only one gun and one cartridge. From delightfully listening to their quiet domestic scufflings, subdued by the fear of blazing day and the proximity of hunters, to being deafened and paralysed by their majestic roars of possession and challenge at mid-night on a tropical stormy night. These experiences have all made their various indelible impressions, but for sheer sustained, intoxicating excitement, the memory of which I can never forget, the following account crowns all to me.

We were away visiting on the Congo River when lions were announced away over the plains. About four o'clock in the afternoon, taking two good boys and a second gun, I went to look for them, hoping to get a glimpse of any that were early risers, adventurously taking an early evening stroll before sunset.

We skirted the open plain, hugging the shade and cover afforded by the numerous anthills, beds of reeds and rank growth. This gave us the double advantage of not being too easily seen and the possibility of stumbling across any lazy lion laid up near its kill. We stumbled and sweated along but drew an absolute blank, so as the sun got low and red we set about to retrace our steps, the tension of concentration becoming greater as the darkness deepened. Just as it was too dark to see to shoot effectively, we struck a narrow village-to-village Native path and then let loose our pent up feelings in voluble conversation and laughter. I handed my .303 rifle to the gun boy ahead, who carried it as usual over his shoulder, with the butt end to the rear, so as to be in instant reach of my hand. The boy with the shotgun came on behind. We all stumbled along hilariously in the gloom. Suddenly, looking to one side of the path and a little ahead, I saw the huge head and shoulders of a crouching lioness. Snatching the rifle off the boy's shoulder, I took a rapid snap shot and hit the beast in the chest. Neither of the boys had seen it, the first boy, dragged back by the gun and the back boy coming on, both fell on me as the gun cracked and the lion grunted. The huge beast took one terrified leap into the air, so that we lost sight of her and wondered when and where she was going to come down. Bewildered, the boys clung onto me as she crashed down into a wee bush not two paces away, and a second shot that showed a blaze in the dark made her change direction and retreat into the bush. It was the first and only time in my whole hunting career that I have seen the animal before my boys. Their eyesight and instincts are wonderful, always making me feel like a pigmy among giants, but this time the gloom gave me the advantage as the light tawny head and shoulders showed lighter in contrast to the dark bush.

We made a noisy and excited return to the village, sleeping very little that night as we planned our return visit to the scene of the lioness at the first streak of dawn. Somewhere about five o'clock the next morning we stood where the beast had given us the shock. First we tracked backwards to where the lioness had come from, and found the newly killed and very slightly eaten carcase of a male lechwe antelope; evidently the lioness had been alone and had just made her kill, and then, being an inquisitive female, disturbed by our talk and laughter, had left her kill to investigate the intruders by lying in wait. Returning we soon found her retreating blood spoor, for she had not gone far, her wound making her lay down frequently. We found ourselves on the edge of a big swamp, where the reeds grew in thick patches, divided only by narrow passages of short scrub, making ideal hiding but impossible hunting country. Bloodthirsty mosquitoes greeted us in clouds. The boys got the first glimpse of her as she made a silent back door exit move to the swamp; another two such moves and she would be absolutely lost to us, so I circled into the swamp myself, motioning the boys away to watch for any retreat on the plain side. As the boys were making their noise on the far side, I just saw the lioness belly crawl across the narrow scrub passage between two islands of twelve feet tall reeds, her retreat being still in the same direction, so I silently took up my place within two paces of what I considered her next move and my last chance. Crouching in this narrow passage, partly hidden behind a tuft of papyrus, with the wind favourable to me, for a solid hour I was eaten alive by mosquitoes. I dare not move, for the slightly agitated reed tops showed me how near the lioness was. My eyes were excitedly glued on the slender reed tops that moved almost imperceptibly, but assured me that she was still there and that inch by inch was creeping towards me. The boys, absolutely sure that I had made a mistake, started throwing into the reed island pieces of ant-hill, and then spears and insulting provoking shouts. They approached so near that my big fear was that some of them would get a mauling, whilst I dare not warn them for fear of revealing my presence. Then, again I saw the reed tops move slightly, and this time right on the edge of the island, breathlessly, I brought my rifle to the aim and waited. Oh, the intoxicating bliss, as at two paces only, I watched first her nose then her eyes and head almost motionlessly coming out of the heavy reeds. Then her neck and shoulders upon which I fired a heart shot. It was a simultaneous shock to the lioness, myself and the now careless Natives; she gave one awful gruntish roar as she reared up on her hind legs, looking like a huge cow. She towered above the tall reeds and falling backwards on top of the abusive Natives, scattered them in all directions shrieking loudly.

She was stone dead and measured up as fine a lioness as ever was seen along the Congo River.

Later thinking over the whole affair and checking up every move, I came to the conclusion that the laying in and smelling of her own blood overnight had cooled off all her courage but had sharpened herself preservation instincts. In my experience, lions are like humans and not true to type, for I have known an unprovoked lioness attack and kill humans, whilst another with cubs would not even stay to protect them, her own offspring, from capture.

9

SOME STRANGE TRUE STORIES OF
ENCOUNTERS WITH BUFFALOES

Of wild animals considered dangerous to the hunter the elephant is, of course, the most impressive; but after the lion, the buffalo is certainly the most dangerous because it is so tenacious to life. Wounded, he becomes wickedly cunning, and lures the hunter into the long grass or dense bush, where, unseen, he circles round on his own tracks to await, with great patience, the coming of the unsuspecting hunter who, all concentration, is following the blood spoor leading so obviously ahead. Then this ton of pent-up cunning, this savage, horned fury, charges him like an avalanche from apparently nowhere. Following a wounded buffalo in long grass or thick bush is as nerve-racking and thrilling as the keenest sportsman can desire.

Before becoming interested in lions, I tried my hand in shooting many buffaloes, and on at least four occasions only Providence saved me from a shocking death. I was never allowed to underestimate these huge beasts, for during my first year in the Congo my two best Native hunting friends were both killed by buffaloes. The one, with over one hundred to his credit, was found dead and mangled alongside the record bull ever shot in this territory. The other, a son of the local chief, a big, handsome fellow and superb hunter of big game, shot and wounded the same old bull four times on four successive days, and each time only just escaped death by a few inches as he scrambled into the tree before the charging buffalo hit it. On the fifth day he got his shot in again, but was just a split-second too late in getting up the tree. The enraged beast crushed his dangling leg, dropped him from the tree, and then pulped him to death before he himself laid down to die of his wounds.

One day, not long afterwards, I followed the spoor of a huge solitary buffalo bull. He took me up hill and down dale for hours before I came up with him as he lay in fairly long grass. My two boys retreated quietly, to climb to safety into a tree, whilst I, making sure of the wind, advanced slowly and quietly, against the breeze, getting nearer and nearer, for I could only see the big black form lying down, and I wanted to find a vulnerable part of his anatomy. At fifteen yards I pulled up, still not knowing which way he lay, so decided to shoot in the middle with the preliminary shot to get him onto his feet and then to get in my vital shot before he realised what had hit him. I took aim and pressed the trigger, but nothing happened, except that the infuriated beast stood up, alarmed at the metallic click.

I dare not look down, and could neither open the bolt nor press the trigger. Not thinking at the time of the danger, I was furiously angry at such a huge target almost on top of me and not being able to get the rifle to crack after so many hours of stalking. The wind was still favourable, and I was indeed fortunate, for the buffalo neither saw nor scented me as he made off into the wind. Then I was able to look down and examine my rifle, and, on doing so, found that the simplest thing had happened, the bolt knob had lifted a little, so that when fired, the bolt only went half-cock and so locked itself. All I got out of that strenuous day's hunt was a bad dose of black-water fever and my two boys sick of either exertion or fright.

Another time I came across a big buffalo bull, but could not get a good shot as he was half hidden behind a huge tree trunk. Getting as near as I thought safe with a small rifle, I took aim. The beast just moved round, facing me, slowly sinking down onto its knees, with its huge horns thrown back on its neck and its nose  scenting the wind in my direction. He looked like making serious trouble for us. I stepped out nearer, into a more favourable spot, so as to get a killing shot, but as I did so one of my boys suddenly lost his head, and throwing his arms around me, tried to drag me back to safety. In front of this huge buffalo we wrestled like mad men, and I had to call another boy to help me to get free or we would all get killed. With heart still palpitating I did get in a brain shot, and then found that my first shot had been our salvation, for it had broken his back, making him unable to charge even when given such an opportunity.

On yet another occasion leaving home at four in the morning, I had come up with a herd of buffaloes about eight o'clock and was greatly surprised to see an odd red Congo buffalo running with the herd of black ones. The Native regards the red one as a buffalo. I soon got near enough without being seen or scented to give the red one a heart shot. Having only a small bore rifle, and knowing how long it takes for a heart shot from such a rifle to take effect, I sat down as usual to take a drink from my water-bottle and enjoy a sandwich, but this time I had to get up, for the red fellow was looking round for me and causing a tremendous commotion amongst the trees. Whilst he was looking my way I got in a throat shot, and then he started coming for me, but fortunately was too wounded for a speedy charge. I got two more chest shots, and then the cartridges in my magazine jammed, so that the rifle was useless and the buffalo was still coming on. My boys were yelling and screaming in the distance. Anyway, just at three yards distance, the huge red beast dropped on his knees, his wounds proving too much for him, although he did try so hard to get up and finish me off. In the meanwhile I managed to slip a loose cartridge into the breach and deliver the death shot.

Another time after a three-hour trek, I came upon a herd of buffalo and, choosing the biggest bull who was looking my way, I gave him a chest shot that came out under his belly and shattered one of his back legs at the knee. Going on three legs, he led me on a dance for over five hours, through the most rough and impossible country, trampling every spot of water en route into filthy stinking mud so that we could not drink, and we were in great distress before we came up with him.

There was a big stretch of long grass which had missed the burn-off, and as the spoor led that way I was sure that the buffalo was waiting there for me, so, knowing that it was he or me for it now, I decided to advance as cautiously and slowly as possible. I brought our "aviation" to bear by sending one hunting boy to climb the first tree and from there examine the ground to the next tree, in order that we might go surely from tree to tree. The boy looked hard and long and reported "Nothing". But just as he looked down to make sure of his footing to descend, he got the shock of his life to see the wounded bull just near the base of the tree.

Throwing some dust in the air, I found the strength and direction of the wind, then signaling my boys back to safety, I cautiously approached against the wind to within three yards of my quarry, and then took careful aim for the brain, but alas, nothing happened, as there was no cartridge in the breech. I had opened and shut the bolt, but the cartridge had not risen from the magazine.

I shall never forget the terrible appearance of the huge beast, all covered with blood and mud, as he loomed almost on top of me. I was like he had just been - too near to be seen - so he charged all right, but in the wrong direction, and I was able to get him down and out with the next shot before he got clear away.

Now my profound thanks to Providence are only equaled by my deepest respect for the buffalo in his own wild country.

10
MY FIGHT WITH A DEMON LION

I was traveling up the river, as usual, to visit all the villages in my scattered parish. At the time, I was far too keen on my own special business to be interested in animals or hunting. Only a very wild, dangerous beast could have excited my interest just then.

Arriving at one of the smaller villages, I soon sensed an ominous silence and fear pervading the place. Believing that I could learn more by listening than by direct questioning, I took my camp chair and sat with the village Natives well away from my own people, pretending to be absorbed in a book. The ruse worked well, and soon they continued their quiet conversations about the exploits and audacity of a "demon" lion that was encroaching daily on the village reservations. I listened long enough to gather the information that an unusually cheeky lion, fearing nothing and yet feared by all the hunter, was terrorising the district. He had taken to a hunting ground not far from the village, but he was impudent and lazy enough to let the Natives do all the hunting and killing for him. As soon as they dropped an antelope, he would walk off with it. He never ran or hid from any one, but made everyone else run and hide from him. This, to me, was most unusual, because I had known these men often chase the lions off their own kill and take the meat.

Having made sure of the facts, I went and spoke to my own local "boy", who was a tall, lanky fisherman. He was genuinely distressed when I told him that I was going after the lion in the morning.

He himself had suddenly developed a very great respect for all wild animals. A hippo had chased him almost to destruction on the riverbank, and the same week another had attacked him while coming downstream with his canoe fully loaded with fish. He lost his canoe and fish, only saving his life by a hasty scramble up the river bank to terrafirma. In trying to dissuade me, he pleaded that everybody knew the lion to be demon-possessed and too cunning to be killed. After a little ridicule and a lot of persuasion, he decided to be my guide to the lion's rendezvous as long as he could be the last man in the file. He thought he would surely be safe enough behind two men and two guns--and his legs were the longest.

I had with me a good boy, who was an accomplished hunter himself and accustomed to lions and my shotgun. He had great faith in me and my old Lee-Metford rifle, so he was willing enough to come on the hunt. At daybreak we set off from the village, taking every precaution as to wind, approach and cover. I rather like cheeky, fearless animals, as they don't waste your time in looking for, and running after, them. This lion was cheeky enough to do the looking himself.

With a roar of defiance, he came right into the open on the roadside, and I got in my first shot, a good hit in the chest. I felt encouraged enough to follow him, and he felt discouraged enough to retire to country more suitable for attack. I was surprised by his big size and the fact that he had no mane.

After a long spell of cautious spooring, the lion gave way his own position by a low, angry growl. It was only a fleeting glimpse I got of him in the long grass, but just enough to get in another chest shot that just reached its mark.

The boys, encouraged by the lion's retreat and the big blood spoor it left behind, started to follow more quickly. Coming to an open space the boy with the shotgun deployed away to the right. Suddenly, I heard an awful yell of fear, and then saw the boy racing for me with the bleeding lion after him. The lion, coming on obliquely, gave me a good chance of a shot, which hit the animal in the shoulder region. It was sufficient and just in time to change his charge into a retreat.

The boy was scared stiff; he said, "Bwana, you have saved my life, for just as you fired all had gone black before my eyes." After that we followed more cautiously. Coming to one tremendous pool of blood, we wondered how the lion could have lain there. On looking up, we were amazed and alarmed to see that the lion had actually climbed up the tree to await our arrival. Our cautious approach had so delayed our arrival that the animal, uncomfortable and bleeding freely, could wait no longer. The lion had leapt down and taken cover at the base of a well-grassed anthill not far away. From there we could hear his laborious and heavy breathing, punctuated with spasms of coughing and vomiting of blood. We truly believed that it was his end and that he would never rise again, but at the same time we saw the need for a careful approach.

Seeing a bare anthill favourable for the wind and which would also give us the advantage of a few feet in height to look into the grass, we silently and unseen took up our position behind it. Then the shotgun boy and I quietly climbed up and sat on the top, the angle making it impossible to stand. Even to sit steady enough for shooting, we had to dig in our heels on the lion's side of the anthill.

The lanky Native fisherman, feeling safe with two guns and hearing the sound of the lion vomiting, felt brave enough to approach to what he thought to be a safe distance, and then hurled insults and clods of earth at the lion to make it show itself.

I was straining every faculty to find that telltale black tuft of a switching tail or the revealing black tips of twitching ears in the brown grass. A lion may charge after only once switching its tail in the air; after three switches of its tail, it is sure to charge, but this demon lion charged without even once switching its tail or twitching its ears.

He let the insulting and disturbing Native get confident enough, and then without the slightest warning charged him like a streak of lightning. My rifle cracked on the first sight of him, but it was like shooting at a target on an express train. With head and tail well down, the lion streaked through the grass at an incredible speed. The Native yelled and ran straight for me. In doing so, he hindered any chance of a second shot, as his own lanky body covered the advance of the attacking lion.

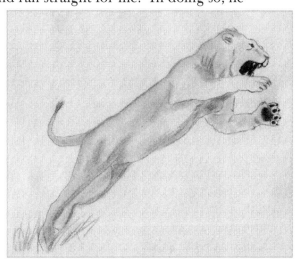

My boy assured me that the

shotgun was charged with buckshot in both barrels, so I dropped my rifle and snatched up the shotgun. Just then, the Native fell flat on the side of the anthill with his outstretched hands trying to grasp my boots and the growling lion on top of him.

Just as the enraged beast was going to sink its huge fangs into the neck or shoulder of the Native, I pushed the shotgun right into its face and pressed both triggers, but nothing happened. It was the biggest shock of my life. Anyway, there must have been something unusually distracting in the smell and touch of that gun barrel, for with its claws still dug into the man's buttocks and back, it lifted up its huge face to mine.

For one brief moment, I gazed right into the blood-streaming jaws of death. It was a paralysing moment that I shall never be able to forget as long as I live.

Suddenly the most amazing thing happened. With a snarl, more of frustration than defiance, he gave one big spit right into my face, then, leaping past me, sat down growling and writhing in the open plain only about twenty paces away. Opening the shotgun, I found two empty shells. The boy in his fright at the first charge of the lion had fired both barrels without knowing that he had done so. Feeling for the rifle, I found it had slid down the anthill out of reach. The wounded Native, howling at the top of his voice, provoked the lion to attempt another charge, which was only stopped just in time by a bullet from the recovered rifle.

The Natives knew more about the beast than I did when they called it a demon lion. Indeed, it was the most wicked devil I ever encountered in lion form. That life-saving leap away into the grass, so sudden and uncalled for, I would rather attribute to Providence than the smell of the gun barrel.

Don't worry about the lanky Native, he soon got better. He did think that another demon lion had got him when I cauterised all his wounds with pure carbolic acid.

11
THE ONLY GOOD CRODOCILES ARE DEAD ONES

"THESE SCALY, MONSTROUS, MAN-TRAPS TAKE A BIGGER TOLL OF LIFE AMONGST THE NATIVE CONGO FISHERMEN THAN ALL THE OTHER WILD ANIMALS PUT TOGETHER, AFTER EVEN THROWING IN THE SERPENTS AS WELL."

Does not the very name crocodile set your teeth on edge or leave a nauseous taste in your mouth? It certainly would if you only knew more of their wicked ways. These scaly, monstrous, mantraps take a bigger toll of life amongst the Native Congo fishermen than all the wild animals put together, after even throwing in the serpents as well. The hardest of men have a soft spot, and the vilest of creatures a redeeming feature somewhere, but I am positively getting sore eyes looking for the crocodile's redeeming feature. It is only absence and distance that can make any heart grow fond of these pre-historic leftovers.

I have never felt so extravagantly charitably disposed to the whole creation of wild life as I do now, and never were my feet less swift to shed blood than at the present time. My softness for animals has come on slowly through experience. At one time, everything moving in the bush was meat for my rifle. Then one day I heard a female antelope piteously cry as I shot it. From that day I vowed never again to shoot a female antelope. Next, a big male antelope that I had shot gave me such a dying look that spoke volumes to my heart, and forever cured me of wanting to shoot anything but dangerous animals. Then a mortally wounded lioness turned her appealing eyes on me and so cut my hunting program down to only marauding and man-eating animals, so there is yet time for the crocodile to find a soft spot in my heart. During these past twenty years, so far he certainly has not, for I still get pleasure in shooting him up on any and every occasion possible, even if he does squeal and cry like a baby when caught. It is the squeal of the coward who does not enjoy his own medicine.

Crocodiles in the big lakes grow to be twenty to thirty feet in length, but ours in this part of the world rarely grow beyond twelve to fifteen feet long. We are blessed, or otherwise, with two different kinds of crocodile here, big black-looking, broad-snouted ones in the rivers, and long narrow-snouted green ones in the lakes. Both sorts are equally keen man-eaters when they get the chance. Perhaps the narrow-nosed one is the less cheeky of the two, but he certainly gets away with more victims than the other, for his rattrap jaws only snap once, and then he drags his prey into deep water to drown. The broad-snouted ones like to open and shut his vile jaws many times on his victim, so occasionally a fighting but badly-lacerated Native is able to save himself, only to die very soon after, unless he receives prompt and professional attendance.

Both kinds, when desperate and hungry enough, will lift Natives right out of their canoes. I had to deal with one man that was taken out of his canoe by one of the broad-nosed ones. The man was a fighter, so whilst the remaining Native paddled off to bring the White man with his gun, he fought the crocodile and hung on to the papyrus. For a full hour the two fought, and in that time the crocodile opened and closed his jaws four times on that poor Native. Very reluctantly he had to let go when help was arriving. The very same crocodile took a Native bathing, and bit him through the arm, the thigh and then almost severed his leg below the knee. I saved his life, and had him going about on crutches, but his own people killed him off when I was out the way, as they had no time for a one-legged man.

Recently my boys hunted and killed a monstrous long-snouted one that had taken one of the boys out of their canoe. They only heard one little cry from the boy and hardly a splash in the water. When the crocodile's carcass was opened, they found the remains of three Natives inside his abominable abysmal depths. His tummy was festering with having swallowed whole legs and feet with hobnailed boots on.

Illustrated by H. Marriott-Burton for "The Outspan" October 27th 1944

It is inconceivable, but absolutely true, that one of these huge reptiles, hatched out, of an egg very little larger than that of a duck, had the audacity to attack a baby elephant whilst it was crossing a channel and tried to get away with it. Of course it paid for its impudence with its life, for the mother elephant, hearing the squeals of her baby, felt around under the water with her trunk, soon found the crocodile, and flung it bodily out onto the bank. Following it up, she crushed it to death with her tusks and knees.

Crocodiles in their craftiness silently and slowly drift into position to make an attack, so that the pursued lechwe or situtungu antelopes manage to cross the channels in safety, whilst the pursuing dogs, lions or man get taken by the crocodile.

Whilst they will attack quite big game from the water, I have only known one case where a crocodile left the water to challenge a lion on its own kill on the riverbank. The two fought to the death, the lion bitten through the shoulder, and the crocodile with its belly ripped open. They even eat their own young and their own wounded species, and are so wicked as to snap their jaws down on the little birds that pick their teeth for them and feast on the irritating flies that halo around the reptile's rotten-smelling mouth and running nose as he basks on the sand bank.

All crocodiles have a passion for rotten meat, and can smell it for miles, so the Natives dig pits in the riverbank and cover them over with grass, then hang up a dead dog for bait. The crocodile in reaching for the over-ripe dog, falls into the pit.

The Native here prizes crocodile meat above any other. Crocodiles often get caught in nets and fish traps, where they do a lot of damage before they drown. Often a man who has lost his wife or child to a crocodile will become a skilled crocodile hunter, harpooning them whilst they are asleep or as they move under water. A crocodile brings a good price, as it is often asked for as a dowry item. The meat looks very much like veal but smells like nothing else on earth, as the Native never cuts up the carcass until its belly is all blown up and the gas permeated all the meat.

There are some witch doctors who can catch crocodiles with hook and line, but the most wicked crocodile that I ever knew was proof against every witch doctor, pit trap and hunter. It had taken so many Natives that the village had been moved three times to get away from the vile

reptile, but he followed them each time. His tactics were to lie up stream, and as soon as anyone approached to draw water, or mostly strangers to call the ferry canoe, then like a flash he would pass, knocking them into the water with his tail. Picking them up in his jaws, he would make off.

When I was in the vicinity, he would keep just out of rifle range. The Chief in desperation offered anything in his village to anyone who would rid him of this plague. When every witchdoctor and hunter had failed, the Chief was going to move the village for the fourth time, my own boy, Tomasi, promised to catch it for him. He was a good Christian, and he took this crocodile's wickedness as a challenge to his own faith.

From the boat he took a nice flexible wire rope, selected the most likely place, and placed his bait and noose, then retired to pray all night in a nearby hut. In the middle of the night the whole village was roused by the most awful squeals and screams, almost human. Turning out, they found the huge crocodile thrashing about in the noose and Tomasi spearing it to death.

What intoxicating joy, and what a hero Tomasi had become overnight! When offered anything in the village, he humbly refused all, saying that the only thing that he really did want was that the old Chief should become a Christian. The old man, with tears in his eyes, could only say, "My lad, you have come too late for that."

The crocodile, when scenting danger, only leaves his two eyes and nose end out of water, so every time I see three knobs on the water like a pawnbroker's sign, I put a bullet in the middle first and make enquiries afterwards, as I now believe, with the Natives, that the only good crocodile is a dead one.

12
FORTY ELEPHANTS AND A MOUSE
(Taken from a recording of a story he told to the children in 1958)

It's lovely when you can talk out of your own experience of what you've seen and known.

In our part of the world, that is central Africa, whilst I am a missionary preaching the gospel, I have had to do more than preach the gospel just by words; I have had to preach it by action in every way. In our part of the world, all of the people look to me to help them, to save them and to deliver them. The government, well, they all refer to me as the lion killer and the spiritual policeman, because all the dangerous animals that nobody will tackle at all, not the government nor the professional hunters or anything, I'm always the one called in to deal with them.

On our lakeside, we have gardens about 20 miles long and about 5 or 6 miles wide, and so it's very very tempting to elephants. The elephants that live on the mountains and over the valleys will come and gather towards the lakeside sometimes. But whilst I'm there they'll just rush in, have a quick meal and off they go back again. Nobody seems to object to that, just now and again.

But at the present time not a lion will come within a mile of anywhere I sleep, and an elephant will not come within two miles - because a lion smells you a mile away and an elephant smells you two miles away and they're sensible to take notice. The only insensible creation are men. All animals, birds, fishes and everything else are sensitive, they know where there's death and keep away, but human beings just walk into it and step in it when they get there.

Well, I was away from the lakeside. I was on the river having a bible school and I was away for some time. So 40 elephants came down onto the lakeside. Well, they had the first meals in the garden and every smell said there was fear everywhere, and since I wasn't there they decided not go home but to come and live on the lakeside until I did come home. So, they feasted in the gardens at night and then in the daytime they came to the lakeside under the big trees and everybody was afraid.

The men had to go to the chief, and the chief and the men all had to go to the government, and the government couldn't do anything at all, even with the soldiers and police and guns and everything.

They just said, "You'll have to go to the missionary."

The men replied, "Well, the elephants are here because the missionary is not here."

So then, the government sends a letter to me - "Will you come and get the 40 elephants off the lakeside for us, because it's famine?"

I just wrote a little letter back and said, "First of all, I'm God's man and I have 3 weeks to go in this bible school yet. I am 120 miles from home. But in 3 weeks time, I'll come back, I'll kill the awful elephants that have taken over and the male that dominated them and I'll guarantee they'll never come back for 12 months."

Well that's the letter I sent back to them and that's what I stuck to, but the elephants knew all about it.

You know we've got television and radio and think we're very clever, but the animal creation had it a long long time ago. Nature, they listen and take in all the messages.

The elephants took it in and said to themselves, "There's no need to worry. That man's not coming back for 3 weeks and everybody else is afraid." And so they settled down, and they just lived on the lakeside, dining in the gardens.

At the end of the 3 weeks I came home. I got home in the afternoon. The elephants never saw me, they never smelled me, and they never heard me. I got in in the afternoon and I called two of my men. I said, "I want you at half past four in the morning. I'll be out to kill the old bull. So you come at half past four in the morning." And so they came. Nobody else heard, only the two men.

But the elephants heard, and that night, they just had a quick meal and they went for dear life - all 40 of them. Right back where they'd come from. The Natives all said, "We knew it would happen". They say they are warned by a dream. They always say that. They always say, "When you come, the night before they are warned in a dream and they get out." Well they did it this night, but it wasn't telepathy, they heard everything.

I went out onto the lakeside and started where the gardens were spoiled. Then I found the elephants were not only walking but running; getting away as fast and as hard as they could. I had to follow them but the wind was blowing from the lake and so they got my scent . Scenting up to two miles away. Every time they'd stop to sniff again and off they went.

I was getting tired. They'd often stop to feed and often stopped to play and so we'd get a chance to catch up with them. But this time they were going too fast. Well, just when we thought we were a long way off and I was getting a bit fed up and wondering when I would catch up to them, I came upon the forest. The forest is not a big one but there were trees all packed together closely, and the tall grass is about 10 feet everywhere. As soon as the elephants got in there they thought there was a bit of safety in the forest. As they got in the forest they did what they couldn't do all night and all morning; the whole lot of them manured.

As soon as I got in the forest the stench was something terrific. There were 40 manure piles all over the place and it was smoking and steaming. I just stood, I told my boys, "Well now it doesn't matter what the wind does, they can never smell us. They've made that much smell themselves, they'll never smell us again." It was steaming reeking everywhere.

Then we moved in a little bit further and I heard an awful noise. It was just like a concrete mixer. It was the old bulls stomach turning over after it's meal and its quick run through the grass. Well when I heard him I said, "Boys, it doesn't matter now what twigs we break and what grass we break and what tree branches. He's making that much noise he'll never hear us. Can't smell us, can't hear us, all we've got to do now is get him. But where is he? The grass is 10 feet tall and he's somewhere about where we can hear him" And so I just stood still and prayed - I didn't close my eyes though. I kept my eyes open and I just prayed and I said "Lord, this old bull is Goliath and I'm little David. I don't want to hurt him and I don't want him to get away wounded. I just want to shoot him once in the eye. It will never hurt him and he drops down stone dead on his knees and rolls over." I'd only just prayed that, just like David, one smack in the eye and it's finished. I'd no sooner just said that when all the cows and the other bulls had gotten away but the old King Bull, he turned around and was looking for me. He couldn't smell me, he couldn't hear me but he knew I was there. And so he came. The big trunk started peering over the top of the grass to get the leaves. When I saw the trunk I followed it down to the head, and the head was behind a big tree. Just as his head came around and his eye came out from behind the tree I just fired one shot, right in the eye. He dropped on his knees, rolled over on his side, stone dead.

Well that was wonderful. It was lovely. God answered prayer just as we'd asked. We never hurt him. He didn't know what had hit him. The others were away and now I could guarantee for 12 months they'd never come back again.

I cut his tail off - that's what you have to do every time with an elephant. You don't need to talk, but all the world just hangs on to every word you've got to say when you've got the tail. I always tell the people, "A tail is a testimony." Natives are not interested in sermons, they don't want to hear about the 39 elephants that got away, they just want to know where this fellow is, where you got his tail, because there's 5 tons of meat.

I told the men "Open his stomach, because we want evidence before the government and everybody else." They opened his stomach and it was full of sweet potatoes. I said, "There's the evidence." The people had come from the garden and people from the village far in the distance. I said to the people, "There's the thief and those the goods upon him." Then I called all the people around and said, "You've not to sell one ounce of this meat; you've not to give any to the Chief, you've not to give any to the government. But it's for you people. It's two days to Christmas, and this is for your Christmas dinner; five tons of meat." Then I said, "Every man, woman and child, wherever they are, whoever can cook it up and carry it away, it's yours free." Now, when you hold the tail they'll never argue, neither chief nor government can argue when you've got the tail there.

The chief wasn't too happy, but I told him "I'm going to give you 50 pounds for your Christmas present. The ivory was worth 100 pounds. The government never gave me anything for it but they gave you 50 pounds at half price. So I'll give it to you for your Christmas present. All I want to take home is this tail and the snapshot that I take." Then I told the people, I said, "You're wailing and sobbing because the animals have eaten the garden but I'm giving you your gardens back second hand. You can eat your garden, but now it's got fat on." And so the people all over the place were really thrilled.

The elephants did get away and they never did come back for one year.

Well, that was the first day.

Now when I got home I was rather surprised and I wondered - because you do wonder. (There's a lot of material things that are not interesting at all, but there are other things that are mighty interesting - God's creation.) So I did ask the Lord, I said, "How is it that forty elephants, weighing 5 tons apiece, defy all the others and then they run away from me and I'm only one little man?"

It was wonderful. All the Natives were thrilled. I tell you, it's better than doing a lot of preaching. When you go in the open air or wherever you go and you find the people wide open. Some of the traders asked the people, "Why have you only got respect for that missionary? You do whatever you like here, but whatever he tells you to do you do it." They replied, "He saved our gardens from famine, he saved our children from dying, he saves us from every terror that comes our way and so whatever he says, we'll do it"
Well, that was wonderful

Later, I was sitting on the lakeside, waiting for a man to come along in the canoe. The heat was terrific at mid-day. It's hot enough any time, but midday there wasn't a breath of wind, it was just like a sun pocket. So I just sat on the edge of the veranda; about eight foot square, with a low roof, sitting on a little deck chair with an antelope skin on and it was awful. Nobody to talk to; there wasn't a man, woman or child around, they'd all gone to sleep in the huts. There wasn't even a dog, they'd all gone under the banana trees, laid on the back of the lake just to keep cool. There wasn't even a hen, they'd all gone and were all stood like this ..... trying to cool off. Not a thing moving anywhere and I was just about fed up. And then, while I was just looking around, there came out of a hole, a mouse. This mouse just came out and stood dazed, looking round, just like ..... that. And I spoke to it.

I said, "You silly little mouse, hide yourself. If anybody but me sees you on this whole lakeside, they'll kill you." Because they kill on sight. The Natives, the children or anybody, there's no mercy for small things. Even the dogs - they never get fed, so they gobble anything, and the hens, they just kill everything. But the mouse just walked around again, looking like this .... and I spoke again "Get out in the dark and hide yourself." (Because I love all little things.) It just ran around the hut, came at my feet, sniffed at my shoes, looked in my face and then ran down its hole. It brought back and put at

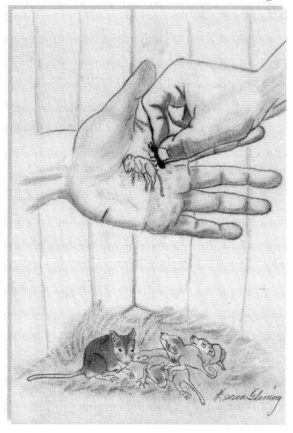

my feet 8 little babies. And it just waited there. The babies were only as big as the top of my thumb. No hair on them, they were only like a ball of meat, but the black ants had got them - the driver ants. So I had to take the driver ants and screw them off, kill them all and wipe the little thing of the blood that it was bleeding. Then I put them all down in a little tuft of grass in the corner, and she settled down with her babies. They were saved.

Well these black ants you know, driver ants, they come along like a great big snake. If they go through the fowl house at night you've only bones left in the morning. If they go through the sheep pen or goat pen - nothing but bones in the morning. Even if you find a wild animal lying down asleep, there's nothing but bones left because they don't get away. And even an elephant; they get up the elephants trunk and bite him until the elephant goes mad, banging his head on the rocks and the trees. Well this rope had come along and it was underground and got her babies, so she came out at midday looking for a saviour for her babies. If anybody else had seen her she would have been killed, yet she came right out to my feet, sniffed, looked, and brought her babies and they were saved.

And I had to say, "Lord, this is too wonderful. 40 elephants, 5 tons apiece, running for dear life to get away, and here's a little mouse, comes and brings her babies that they might be saved."

It is wonderful beloved. I was wondering why, and the Lord just showed me: It's just the same as Jesus. When Jesus was on earth, there was no man more attractive to children. The children gathered around Jesus until the disciples had to tell them to stop it. Jesus said, "Forbid them not, for such is the Kingdom of Heaven." The weakest women who daren't go to a doctor yet crawled and touched the edge of his garment, the poorest beggars, whoever they were, when they were despised by others, there was never one turned away by Jesus and he drew them like a magnet. But every wicked thing, I tell you, they ran away as hard as they could.

Jesus said "I have come to seek and to save that which was lost." And it's only tenderness that can win that which is lost.

So that's my job in Congo and has been the last 38 years; seeking to save that which is lost.

Oh what a priceless privilege!

Printed in Great Britain
by Amazon

66833679R00050